THE VOICE OF THE SILENCE

H.P. Blavatsky

CLASSY
PUBLISHING

THE VOICE OF THE SILENCE
by H.P. Blavatsky
Published by Classy Publishing, 2025

www.classypublishing.com
info@classypublishing.com

ISBN: 978-93-5522-660-0

Cover Image by Milano / Adobe Stock
Cover Design by Classy Publishing

Contents

Contents

Preface

The following pages are derived from "The Book of the Golden Precepts," one of the works put into the hands of mystic students in the East. The knowledge of them is obligatory in that school, the teachings of which are accepted by many Theosophists. Therefore, as I know many of these Precepts by heart, the work of translating has been relatively an easy task for me.

It is well known that, in India, the methods of psychic development differ with the Gurus (teachers or masters), not only because of their belonging to different schools of philosophy, of which there are six, but because every Guru has his own system, which he generally keeps very secret. But beyond the Himalayas the method in the Esoteric Schools does not differ, unless the Guru is simply a Lama, but little more learned than those he teaches.

The work from which I here translate forms part of the same series as that from which the "Stanzas" of the *Book of Dzyan* were taken, on which the *Secret Doctrine* is based.

Together with the great mystic work called *Paramârtha*, which, the legend of *Nâgârjuna* tells us, was delivered to the great Arhat by the Nâgas or "Serpents" (in truth a name given to the ancient Initiates), the "Book of the Golden Precepts" claims the same origin. Yet its maxims and ideas, however noble and original, are often found under different forms in Sanskrit works, such as the *Jñâneśvari*, that superb mystic treatise in which Krishna describes to Arjuna in glowing colours the condition of a fully illumined Yogi; and again in certain Upanishads. This is but natural, since most, if not all, of the greatest Arhats, the first followers of Gautama Buddha were Hindus and Âryans, not Mongolians, especially those who emigrated into Tibet. The works left by Âryâsanga alone are very numerous.

The original *Precepts* are engraved on thin oblong squares; copies very often on discs. These discs, or plates, are generally preserved on the altars of the temples attached to centres where the so-called "contemplative" or Mahâyâna (Yogâchâra) schools are established. They are written variously, sometimes in Tibetan but mostly in ideographs. The sacerdotal language (Senzar), besides an alphabet of its own, may be rendered in several modes of writing in cypher characters, which partake more of the nature of ideographs than of syllables. Another method (*lug*, in Tibetan) is to use the numerals and colours, each of which corresponds to a letter of the Tibetan alphabet (thirty simple and seventy-four compound letters) thus forming a complete cryptographic alphabet. When the ideographs are used there is a definite mode of reading the text; as in this case the symbols and signs used in astrology, namely the twelve zodiacal animals and the seven primary colours, each a triplet in shade, *i.e.* the light, the primary, and the dark—stand for the thirty-three letters of the simple alphabet, for words and sentences. For in this method, the twelve "animals" five times repeated and coupled with the five elements and the seven colours, furnish a whole alphabet composed of sixty sacred letters and twelve signs. A sign placed at the beginning of the text determines whether the reader has to spell it according to the Indian mode, when every word is simply a Sanskrit adaptation, or according to the Chinese principle of reading the ideographs. The easiest way however, is that which allows the reader to use no special, or *any* language he likes, as the signs and symbols were, like the Arabian numerals or figures, common and international property among initiated mystics and their followers. The same peculiarity is characteristic of one of the Chinese modes of writing, which can be read with equal facility by any one acquainted with the character: for instance, a Japanese can read it in his own language as readily as a Chinaman in his.

The Book of the Golden Precepts—some of which are pre-Buddhistic while others belong to a later date—contains about ninety distinct little treatises. Of these I learnt thirty-nine by heart, years ago. To translate the rest, I should have to resort to notes scattered among a too large number of papers and memoranda collected for the last twenty years and never put in order, to make of it by any means an easy task. Nor could they be all translated and given to a world too selfish and too much attached to objects of sense to be in any way prepared to receive such exalted ethics in the right spirit. For, unless a man perseveres seriously in the pursuit of self-knowledge, he will never lend a willing ear to advice of this nature.

And yet such ethics fill volumes upon volumes in Eastern literature, especially in the Upanishads. "Kill out all desire of life," says Krishna to Arjuna. That desire lingers only in the body, the vehicle of the embodied Self, not in the SELF which is "eternal, indestructible, which kills not nor is it killed" (*Katha Upanishad*). "Kill out sensation," teaches *Sutta Nipâta*; "look alike on pleasure and pain, gain and loss, victory and defeat." Again, "Seek shelter in the eternal alone" (*ibid*). "Destroy the sense of separateness," repeats Krishna under every form. "The Mind (*Manas*) which follows the rambling senses, makes the Soul (*Buddhi*) as helpless as the boat which the wind leads astray upon the waters" (*Bhagavadgîtâ* II. 70).

Therefore it has been thought better to make a judicious selection only from those treatises which will best suit the few real mystics in the Theosophical Society, and which are sure to answer their needs. It is only these who will appreciate these words of Krishna-Christos, the "Higher Self":—

"Sages do not grieve for the living nor the dead. Never did I not exist, nor you, nor these rulers of men; nor will any one of us ever hereafter cease to be." (*Bhagavadgîtâ* II. 27).

In this translation, I have done my best to preserve the poetical beauty of language and imagery which characterise the original. How far this effort has been successful, is for the reader to judge.—"H.P. BLAVATSKY."

FRAGMENT I

The Voice of the Silence

These instructions are for those ignorant of the dangers of the lower IDDHI[1].

He who would hear the voice of *Nâda*[2], "the Soundless Sound," and comprehend it, he has to learn the nature of *Dhâranâ*[3].

---

[1] The Pali word *Iddhi*, is the synonym of the Sanskrit *Siddhis*, or psychic faculties, the abnormal powers in man. There are two kinds of *Siddhis*. One group which embraces the lower, coarse, psychic and mental energies; the other is one which exacts the highest training of Spiritual powers. Says Krishna in *Śrîmad Bhâgavatam*:—

"He who is engaged in the performance of yoga, who has subdued his senses and who has concentrated his mind in me (Krishna), such yogis all the Siddhis stand ready to serve."

[2] The "Soundless Voice," or the "Voice of the Silence." *Literally* perhaps this would read "Voice in the *Spiritual Sound*," as *Nâda* is the equivalent word in Sanskrit, for the *Sen-sar* term.

[3] *Dhâranâ*, is the intense and perfect concentration of the mind upon some one interior object, accompanied by complete abstraction from

Having become indifferent to objects of perception, the pupil must seek out the *râja* of the senses, the Thought-Producer, he who awakes illusion.

The Mind is the great Slayer of the Real.

Let the Disciple slay the Slayer.

For: —

When to himself his form appears unreal, as do on waking all the forms he sees in dreams;

When he has ceased to hear the many, he may discern the ONE—the inner sound which kills the outer.

Then only, not till then, shall he forsake the region of *Asat*, the false, to come unto the realm of *Sat*, the true.

Before the soul can see, the Harmony within must be attained, and fleshly eyes be rendered blind to all illusion.

Before the Soul can hear, the image (man) has to become as deaf to roarings as to whispers, to cries of bellowing elephants as to the silvery buzzing of the golden fire-fly.

Before the soul can comprehend and may remember, she must unto the Silent Speaker be united just as the form to

---

everything pertaining to the external Universe, or the world of the senses.

which the clay is modelled, is first united with the potter's mind.

For then the soul will hear, and will remember.

And then to the inner ear will speak—

THE VOICE OF THE SILENCE

And say:—

If thy soul smiles while bathing in the Sunlight of thy Life; if thy soul sings within her chrysalis of flesh and matter; if thy soul weeps inside her castle of illusion; if thy soul struggles to break the silver thread that binds her to the MASTER[4]; know, O Disciple, thy Soul is of the earth.

When to the World's turmoil thy budding soul[5] lends ear; when to the roaring voice of the great illusion thy Soul responds[6]; when frightened at the sight of the hot tears of pain, when deafened by the cries of distress, thy soul withdraws like the shy turtle within the carapace of

---

[4] The "great Master" is the term used by *lanoos* or chelas to indicate one's "Higher Self." It is the equivalent of *Avalokiteśvara*, and the same as *Âdi-Budha* with the Buddhist Occultists, Âtman the "Self" (the Higher Self) with the Brahmins, and Christos with the ancient Gnostics.

[5] Soul is used here for the *Human Ego* or Manas, that which is referred to in our Occult Septenary division as the "Human Soul" (*Vide* the *Secret Doctrine*) in contradistinction to the Spiritual and Animal Souls.

[6] *Mahâ Mâyâ* "Great Illusion," the objective Universe.

SELFHOOD, learn, O Disciple, of her Silent "God," thy Soul is an unworthy shrine.

When waxing stronger, thy Soul glides forth from her secure retreat: and breaking loose from the protecting shrine, extends her silver thread and rushes onward; when beholding her image on the waves of Space she whispers, "This is I,"—declare, O Disciple, that thy soul is caught in the webs of delusion[7].

This Earth, Disciple, is the Hall of Sorrow, wherein are set along the Path of dire probations, traps to ensnare thy EGO by the delusion called "Great Heresy"[8].

This earth, O ignorant Disciple, is but the dismal entrance leading to the twilight that precedes the valley of true light—that light which no wind can extinguish, that light which burns without a wick or fuel.

Saith the Great Law:—"In order to become the knower of ALL SELF[9] thou hast first of self to be the knower." To reach the knowledge of that self, thou hast to give up *Self* to Non-Self, Being to Non-Being, and then thou canst repose between the wings of the GREAT BIRD. Aye, sweet is rest

---

[7] *Sakkâyaditthi* "delusion" of personality.

[8] *Attavâda*, the heresy of the belief in Soul or rather in the separateness of Soul or *Self* from the One Universal, infinite Self.

[9] The *Tattvajñânin* is the "knower" or discriminator of the principles in nature and in man; and *Âtmajñânin* is the knower of Âtman or the Universal, One Self.

between the wings of that which is not born, nor dies, but is the AUM[10] throughout eternal ages[11].

Bestride the Bird of Life, if thou would'st know[12].

Give up thy life, if thou would'st live[13].

Three Halls, O weary pilgrim, lead to the end of toils. Three Halls, O conqueror of Mâra, will bring thee through three states[14] into the fourth[15] and thence into the seven worlds[16], the worlds of Rest Eternal.

---

[10] *Kala Hamsa*, the "Bird" or Swan (*Vide* No. 11). Says the *Nâda-Bindu Upanishad* (Rig Veda) translated by the *Kumbakonam Theos. Society*—"The syllable a is considered to be its (the bird Hamsa's) right wing, u, its left, m, its tail, and the Ardha-mâtra (half metre) is said to be its head."

[11] Eternity with the Orientals has quite another signification than it has with us. It stands generally for the 100 years or "age" of Brahmâ, the duration of a Kalpa or a period of 4,320,000,000 years.

[12] Says the same *Nâda-Bindu*, "A Yogi who bestrides the Hamsa (thus contemplates on Aum) is not affected by Karmic influences or crores of sins."

[13] Give up the life of physical *personality* if you would live in spirit.

[14] The three states of consciousness, which are *Jâgrat*, the waking; *Svapna*, the dreaming; and *Sushupti*, the deep sleeping state. These three *Yogi* conditions, lead to the fourth, or—

[15] The *Turîya*, that beyond the dreamless state, the one above all, a state of high spiritual consciousness.

[16] Some Sanskrit mystics locate seven planes of being, the seven spiritual *lokas* or worlds within the body of *Kala Hamsa*, the Swan out of Time and Space, convertible into the Swan *in* Time, when it becomes Brahmâ instead of Brahma (neuter).

If thou would'st learn their names, then hearken, and remember.

The name of the first Hall is IGNORANCE—*Avidyâ.*

It is the Hall in which thou saw'st the light, in which thou livest and shalt die[17].

The name of Hall the second is the Hall of Learning.[18] In it thy Soul will find the blossoms of life, but under every flower a serpent coiled[19].

The name of the third Hall is Wisdom, beyond which stretch the shoreless waters of AKSHARA, the indestructible Fount of Omniscience[20].

If thou would'st cross the first Hall safely, let not thy mind mistake the fires of lust that burn therein for the Sunlight of life.

If thou would'st cross the second safely, stop not the fragrance of its stupefying blossoms to inhale. If freed

---

[17] The phenomenal World of Senses and of terrestrial consciousness—only.

[18] The Hall of *Probationary* Learning.

[19] The astral region, the Psychic World of super-sensuous perceptions and of deceptive sights—the world of Mediums. It is the great "Astral Serpent" of Éliphas Lévi. No blossom plucked in those regions has ever yet been brought down on earth without its serpent coiled around the stem. It is the world of the *Great Illusion.*

[20] The region of the full Spiritual Consciousness beyond which there is no longer danger for him who has reached it.

thou would'st be from the Karmic chains, seek not for thy Guru in those Mâyâvic regions.

The WISE ONES tarry not in pleasure-grounds of senses.

The WISE ONES heed not the sweet-tongued voices of illusion.

Seek for him who is to give thee birth[21], in the Hall of Wisdom, the Hall which lies beyond, wherein all shadows are unknown, and where the light of truth shines with unfading glory.

That which is uncreate abides in thee, Disciple, as it abides in that Hall. If thou would'st reach it and blend the two, thou must divest thyself of thy dark garments of illusion. Stifle the voice of flesh, allow no image of the senses to get between its light and thine that thus the twain may blend in one. And having learnt thine own *Ajñâna*[22], flee from the Hall of Learning. This Hall is dangerous in its perfidious beauty, is needed but for thy probation. Beware, Lanoo, lest dazzled by illusive radiance thy Soul should linger and be caught in its deceptive light.

This light shines from the jewel of the Great Ensnarer, (Mâra)[23]. The senses it bewitches, blinds the mind, and leaves the unwary an abandoned wreck.

---

[21] The Initiate who leads the disciple through the Knowledge given to him to his spiritual, or second, birth is called the *Father* guru or Master.

[22] *Ajñâna* is ignorance or *non*-wisdom the opposite of "Knowledge," *jñâna*.

[23] *Mâra* is in exoteric religions a demon, an *Asura*, but in esoteric philosophy it is personified temptation through men's vices, and

The moth attracted to the dazzling flame of thy night-lamp is doomed to perish in the viscid oil. The unwary Soul that fails to grapple with the mocking demon of illusion, will return to earth the slave of Mâra.

Behold the Hosts of Souls. Watch how they hover o'er the stormy sea of human life, and how exhausted, bleeding, broken-winged, they drop one after other on the swelling waves. Tossed by the fierce winds, chased by the gale, they drift into the eddies and disappear within the first great vortex.

If through the Hall of Wisdom, thou would'st reach the Vale of Bliss, Disciple, close fast thy senses against the great dire heresy of separateness that weans thee from the rest.

Let not thy "Heaven-born," merged in the sea of Mâyâ, break from the Universal Parent (SOUL), but let the fiery power retire into the inmost chamber, the chamber of the Heart[24] and the abode of the World's Mother[25].

---

translated literally means "that which kills" the Soul. It is represented as a King (of the Mâras) with a crown in which shines a jewel of such lustre that it blinds those who look at it, this lustre referring of course to the fascination exercised by vice upon certain natures.

[24] The *inner* chamber of the Heart, called in Sanskrit *Brahmapura.* The "fiery power" is Kundalinî.

[25] The "Power" and the "World-mother" are names given to Kundalinî—one of the mystic "Yogi powers." It is *Buddhi* considered as an active instead of a passive principle (which it is generally, when regarded only as the vehicle, or casket of the Supreme Spirit Âtma). It is an electro-spiritual force, a creative power which when aroused into action can as easily kill as it can create.

Then from the heart that Power shall rise into the sixth, the middle region, the place between thine eyes, when it becomes the breath of the ONE-SOUL, the voice which filleth all, thy Master's voice.

'Tis only then thou canst become a "Walker of the Sky"[26] who treads the winds above the waves, whose step touches not the waters.

Before thou set'st thy foot upon the ladder's upper rung, the ladder of the mystic sounds, thou hast to hear the voice of thy *inner* GOD[27] in seven manners.

The first is like the nightingale's sweet voice chanting a song of parting to its mate.

The second comes as the sound of a silver cymbal of the Dhyânis, awakening the twinkling stars.

The next is as the plaint melodious of the ocean-sprite imprisoned in its shell.

And this is followed by the chant of Vînâ[28].

---

[26] *Khechara* or "sky-walker" or "goer." As explained in the 6th *Adhyâya* of that king of mystic works the *Jñâneśvari*—the body of the Yogi becomes as one *formed of the wind*; as "a cloud from which limbs have sprouted out," after which—"he (the Yogi) beholds the things beyond the seas and stars; he hears the language of the Devas and comprehends it, and perceives what is passing in the mind of the ant."

[27] The Higher SELF.

[28] *Vînâ* is an Indian stringed instrument like a lute.

The fifth like sound of bamboo-flute shrills in thine ear.

It changes next into a trumpet-blast.

The last vibrates like the dull rumbling of a thunder-cloud.

The seventh swallows all the other sounds. They die, and then are heard no more.

When the six[29] are slain and at the Master's feet are laid, then is the pupil merged into the ONE[30], becomes that ONE and lives therein.

Before that path is entered, thou must destroy thy lunar body[31], cleanse thy mind-body[32] and make clean thy heart.

Eternal life's pure waters, clear and crystal, with the monsoon tempest's muddy torrents cannot mingle.

Heaven's dew-drop glittering in the morn's first sun-beam within the bosom of the lotus, when dropped on earth becomes a piece of clay; behold, the pearl is now a speck of mire.

---

[29] The six principles; meaning when the lower personality is destroyed and the inner individuality is merged into and lost in the Seventh or Spirit.

[30] The disciple is one with Brahmâ or the Âtman.

[31] The astral form produced by the *Kâmic* principle, the *Kâma rûpa* or body of desire.

[32] *Mânasa rûpa*. The first refers to the astral or *personal* Self; the second to the individuality or the reincarnating *Ego* whose consciousness on our plane or the *lower Manas*—has to be paralyzed.

Strive with thy thoughts unclean before they overpower thee. Use them as they will thee, for if thou sparest them and they take root and grow, know well, these thoughts will overpower and kill thee. Beware, Disciple, suffer not, e'en though it be their shadow, to approach. For it will grow, increase in size and power, and then this thing of darkness will absorb thy being before thou hast well realized the black foul monster's presence.

Before the "mystic Power"[33*] can make of thee a god, Lanoo, thou must have gained the faculty to slay thy lunar form at will.

The Self of matter and the SELF of Spirit can never meet. One of the twain must disappear; there is no place for both.

Ere thy Soul's mind can understand, the bud of personality must be crushed out, the worm of sense destroyed past resurrection.

Thou canst not travel on the Path before thou hast become that Path itself[34].

---

[33] *Kundalinî* (the "Serpent Power" or mystic fire.) is called the "Serpentine" or the *annular* power on account of its spiral-like working or progress in the body of the ascetic developing the power in himself. It is an electric fiery occult or *Fohatic* power, the great pristine force, which underlies all organic and inorganic matter.

[34] This "Path" is mentioned in all the Mystic Works. As Krishna says in the *Jñâneśvari*: "When this Path is beheld...whether one sets out to the bloom of the east or to the chambers of the west, *without moving*, O holder of the bow, *is the travelling in this road.* In this path, to whatever

Let thy Soul lend its ear to every cry of pain like as the lotus bares its heart to drink the morning sun.

Let not the fierce Sun dry one tear of pain before thyself hast wiped it from the sufferer's eye.

But let each burning human tear drop on thy heart and there remain, nor ever brush it off, until the pain that caused it is removed.

These tears, O thou of heart most merciful, these are the streams that irrigate the fields of charity immortal. 'Tis on such soil that grows the midnight blossom of Buddha[35] more difficult to find, more rare to view than is the flower of the Vogay tree. It is the seed of freedom from rebirth. It isolates the Arhat both from strife and lust, it leads him through the fields of Being unto the peace and bliss known only in the land of Silence and Non-Being.

Kill out desire; but if thou killest it take heed lest from the dead it should again arise.

Kill love of life, but if thou slayest *tanhâ*[36], let this not be for thirst of life eternal, but to replace the fleeting by the everlasting.

---

place one would go, *that place one's own self* becomes." "Thou art the Path" is said to the adept guru and by the latter to the disciple, after initiation. "I am the way and the Path" says another Master.

[35] Adeptship—the "blossom of *Bodhisattva*."

[36] *Tanhâ*—"the will to live," the fear of death and love for life, that force or energy which causes the rebirths.

Desire nothing. Chafe not at Karma, nor at Nature's changeless laws. But struggle only with the personal, the transitory, the evanescent and the perishable.

Help Nature and work on with her; and Nature will regard thee as one of her creators and make obeisance.

And she will open wide before thee the portals of her secret chambers, lay bare before thy gaze the treasures hidden in the very depths of her pure virgin bosom. Unsullied by the hand of matter she shows her treasures only to the eye of Spirit—the eye which never closes, the eye for which there is no veil in all her kingdoms.

Then will she show thee the means and way, the first gate and the second, the third, up to the very seventh. And then, the goal—beyond which lie, bathed in the sunlight of the Spirit, glories untold, unseen by any save the eye of Soul.

There is but one road to the Path; at its very end alone the "Voice of the Silence" can be heard. The ladder by which the candidate ascends is formed of rungs of suffering and pain; these can be silenced only by the voice of virtue. Woe, then, to thee, Disciple, if there is one single vice thou hast not left behind. For then the ladder will give way and overthrow thee; its foot rests in the deep mire of thy sins and failings, and ere thou canst attempt to cross this wide abyss of matter thou hast to lave thy feet in Waters of Renunciation. Beware lest thou should'st set a foot still soiled upon the ladder's lowest rung. Woe unto him who dares pollute one rung with miry feet. The foul and viscous mud will dry, become tenacious, then glue his feet unto the spot, and like a bird caught in the wily fowler's lime, he will be stayed from further progress. His vices will take shape and drag him down. His sins will raise their voices like as the jackal's laugh and sob after the sun goes down; his thoughts become an army, and bear him off a captive slave.

Kill thy desires, Lanoo, make thy vices impotent, ere the first step is taken on the solemn journey.

Strangle thy sins, and make them dumb for ever, before thou dost lift one foot to mount the ladder.

Silence thy thoughts and fix thy whole attention on thy Master whom yet thou dost not see, but whom thou feelest.

Merge into one sense thy senses, if thou would'st be secure against the foe. 'Tis by that sense alone which lies concealed within the hollow of thy brain, that the steep path which leadeth to thy Master may be disclosed before thy Soul's dim eyes.

Long and weary is the way before thee, O Disciple. One single thought about the past that thou hast left behind, will drag thee down and thou wilt have to start the climb anew.

Kill in thyself all memory of past experiences. Look not behind or thou art lost.

Do not believe that lust can ever be killed out if gratified or satiated, for this is an abomination inspired by Mâra. It is by feeding vice that it expands and waxes strong, like to the worm that fattens on the blossom's heart.

The rose must re-become the bud born of its parent stem, before the parasite has eaten through its heart and drunk its life-sap.

The golden tree puts forth its jewel-buds before its trunk is withered by the storm.

The pupil must regain *the child-state he has lost* 'ere the first sound can fall upon his ear.

The light from the ONE Master, the one unfading golden light of Spirit, shoots its effulgent beams on the disciple from the very first. Its rays thread through the thick dark clouds of matter.

Now here, now there, these rays illumine it, like sun-sparks light the earth through the thick foliage of the jungle growth. But, O Disciple, unless the flesh is passive, head cool, the soul as firm and pure as flaming diamond, the radiance will not reach the *chamber*[37], its sunlight will not warm the heart, nor will the mystic sounds of the Âkâśic heights[38] reach the ear, however eager, at the initial stage.

---

[37] The *inner* chamber of the Heart, called in Sanskrit *Brahmapura.* The "fiery power" is Kundalinî.

[38] These mystic sounds or the melody heard by the ascetic at the beginning of his cycle of meditation called *Anâhata-śabda* by the Yogis.

Unless thou hearest, thou canst not see.

Unless thou seest thou canst not hear. To hear and see this is the second stage.

* * *

When the disciple sees and hears, and when he smells and tastes, eyes closed, ears shut, with mouth and nostrils stopped; when the four senses blend and ready are to pass into the fifth, that of the inner touch—then into stage the fourth he hath passed on.

And in the fifth, O slayer of thy thoughts, all these again have to be killed beyond reanimation[39].

Withhold thy mind from all external objects, all external sights. Withhold internal images, lest on thy Soul-light a dark shadow they should cast.

Thou art now in DHÂRANÂ[40], the sixth stage.

When thou hast passed into the seventh, O happy one, thou shalt perceive no more the sacred three[41], for thou

---

[39] This means that in the sixth stage of development which, in the occult system is *Dhâranâ*, every sense as an individual faculty has to be "killed" (or paralyzed) on this plane, passing into and merging with the *Seventh* sense, the most spiritual.

[40] *Dhâranâ*, is the intense and perfect concentration of the mind upon some one interior object, accompanied by complete abstraction from everything pertaining to the external Universe, or the world of the senses.

[41] Every stage of development in *Râja Yoga* is symbolised by a geometrical figure. This one is the sacred *Triangle* and precedes

shalt have become that three thyself. Thyself and mind, like twins upon a line, the star which is thy goal, burns overhead[42]. The three that dwell in glory and in bliss ineffable, now in the world of Mâyâ have lost their names. They have become one star, the fire that burns but scorches not, that fire which is the Upâdhi[43] of the Flame.

And this, O Yogi of success, is what men call Dhyâna[44], the right precursor of Samâdhi[45].

Dhâranâ. The [triangle] is the sign of the high chelas, while another kind of triangle is that of high Initiates. It is the symbol "I" discoursed upon by Buddha and used by him as a symbol of the embodied form of Tathâgata when released from the three methods of the *Prajñâ.* Once the preliminary and lower stages passed, the disciple sees no more the [triangle] but the—the abbreviation of the—, the full Septenary. *Its true form is not given here, as it is almost sure to be pounced upon by some charlatans and*—desecrated in its use for fraudulent purposes.

42 The star that burns overhead is the "the star of initiation." The caste-mark of Śaivas, or devotees of the sect of Śiva, the great patron of all Yogins, is a black round spot, the symbol of the *Sun* now, perhaps, but that of the star of initiation, in Occultism, in days of old.

43 The *basis* (*upâdhi*) of the ever unreachable "flame," so long as the ascetic is still in this life.

44 *Dhyâna* is the last stage before the final *on this Earth* unless one becomes a full mahatma. As said already in this state the Râja Yogi is yet spiritually conscious of Self, and the working of his higher principles. One step more, and he will be on the plane beyond the Seventh (or fourth according to some schools). These, after the practice of *Pratyâhâra*—a preliminary training, in order to control one's mind and thoughts—count Dhâranâ, Dhyâna and Samâdhi and embraces the three under the generic name of Samyama.

45 *Samâdhi* is the state in which the ascetic loses the consciousness of every individuality including his own. He becomes—the All.

And now thy *Self* is lost in SELF, *thyself* unto THYSELF, merged in THAT SELF from which thou first didst radiate.

Where is thy individuality, Lanoo, where the Lanoo himself? It is the spark lost in the fire, the drop within the ocean, the ever-present Ray become the all and the eternal radiance.

And now, Lanoo, thou art the doer and the witness, the radiator and the radiation, Light in the Sound, and the Sound in the Light.

Thou art acquainted with the five impediments, O blessed one. Thou art their conqueror, the Master of the sixth, deliverer of the four modes of Truth[46]. The light that falls upon them shines from thyself, O thou who wast disciple but art Teacher now.

And of these modes of Truth:—

Hast thou not passed through knowledge of all misery—Truth the first?

Hast thou not conquered the Mâras' King at Tsi, the portal of assembling—truth the second?[47].

---

[46] The "four modes of truth" are, in Northern Buddhism, *Ku* "suffering or misery"; *Tu* the assembling of temptations; *Mu* "their destructions" and *Tao*, the "path." The "five impediments" are the knowledge of misery, truth about human frailty, oppressive restraints, and the absolute necessity of separation from all the ties of passion and even of desires. The "Path of Salvation"—is the last one.

[47] At the portal of the "assembling" the King of the Mâras the *Mahâ Mâra* stands trying to blind the candidate by the radiance of his "Jewel."

Hast thou not sin at the third gate destroyed and truth the third attained?

Hast not thou entered *Tao*, "the Path" that leads to knowledge—the fourth truth?[48].

And now, rest 'neath the Bodhi tree, which is perfection of all knowledge, for, know, thou art the Master of SAMÂDHI—the state of faultless vision.

Behold! thou hast become the light, thou hast become the Sound, thou art thy Master and thy God. Thou art THYSELF the object of thy search: the VOICE unbroken, that resounds throughout eternities, exempt from change, from sin exempt, the seven sounds in one, the

VOICE OF THE SILENCE

Om Tat Sat

---

[48] This is the fourth "Path" out of the five paths of rebirth which lead and toss all human beings into perpetual states of sorrow and joy. These "paths" are but subdivisions of the One, the Path followed by Karma.

FRAGMENT II

The Two Paths

And now, O Teacher of Compassion, point thou the way to other men. Behold, all those who knocking for admission, await in ignorance and darkness, to see the gate of the Sweet Law flung open!

The voice of the Candidates:

Shalt not thou, Master of thine own Mercy, reveal the Doctrine of the Heart?[49] Shalt thou refuse to lead thy Servants unto the Path of Liberation?

---

[49] The two schools of Buddha's doctrine, the esoteric and the exoteric, are respectively called the "Heart" and the "Eye" Doctrine. Bodhidharma called them in China—from whence the names reached Tibet—the *Tsung-men* (esoteric) and *Kiau-men* (exoteric school). It is so named, because it is the teaching which emanated from Gautama Buddha's *heart*, whereas the "Eye" Doctrine was the work of his head or brain. The "Heart Doctrine" is also called "the seal of truth" or the "true seal," a symbol found on the heading of almost all esoteric works.

Quoth the Teacher:

The Paths are two; the great Perfections three; six are the Virtues that transform the body into the Tree of Knowledge[50].

Who shall approach them?

Who shall first enter them?

Who shall first hear the doctrine of two Paths in one, the truth unveiled about the Secret Heart?[51] The Law which, shunning learning, teaches Wisdom, reveals a tale of woe.

Alas, alas, that all men should possess Alaya, be one with the great Soul, and that possessing it, Alaya should so little avail them!

Behold how like the moon, reflected in the tranquil waves, Alaya is reflected by the small and by the great, is mirrored in the tiniest atoms, yet fails to reach the heart of all. Alas, that so few men should profit by the gift, the priceless boon of learning truth, the right perception of existing things, the Knowledge of the non-existent!

---

[50] The "tree of knowledge" is a title given by the followers of the *Bodhidharma* (Wisdom religion) to those who have attained the height of mystic knowledge—adepts. Nâgârjuna the founder of the Mâdhyamika School was called the "Dragon Tree," Dragon standing as a symbol of Wisdom and Knowledge. The tree is honoured because it is under the Bodhi (wisdom) Tree that Buddha received his birth and enlightenment, preached his first sermon and died.

[51] "Secret Heart" is the esoteric doctrine.

Saith the pupil:

O Teacher, what shall I do to reach to Wisdom?

O Wise one, what, to gain perfection?

Search for the Paths. But, O Lanoo, be of clean heart before thou startest on thy journey. Before thou takest thy first step learn to discern the real from the false, the ever-fleeting from the everlasting. Learn above all to separate Head-learning from Soul-Wisdom, the "Eye" from the "Heart" doctrine.

Yea, ignorance is like unto a closed and airless vessel; the soul a bird shut up within. It warbles not, nor can it stir a feather; but the songster mute and torpid sits, and of exhaustion dies.

But even ignorance is better than Head-learning with no Soul-wisdom to illuminate and guide it.

The seeds of Wisdom cannot sprout and grow in airless space. To live and reap experience the mind needs breadth and depth and points to draw it towards the Diamond Soul[52]. Seek not those points in *Mâyâ's* realm; but soar beyond illusions, search the eternal and the changeless sat[53], mistrusting fancy's false suggestions.

---

[52] "Diamond Soul" "Vajrasattva," a title of the supreme Buddha, the "Lord of all Mysteries," called Vajradhara and Âdi-Buddha.

[53] Sat, the one eternal and Absolute Reality and Truth, all the rest being illusion.

For mind is like a mirror; it gathers dust while it reflects[54]. It needs the gentle breezes of Soul-Wisdom to brush away the dust of our illusions. Seek O Beginner, to blend thy Mind and Soul.

Shun ignorance, and likewise shun illusion. Avert thy face from world deceptions; mistrust thy senses, they are false. But within thy body—the shrine of thy sensations—seek in the Impersonal for the "eternal man"[55]; and having sought him out, look inward: thou art Buddha[56].

Shun praise, O Devotee. Praise leads to self-delusion. Thy body is not self, thy self is in itself without a body, and either praise or blame affects it not.

Self-gratulation, O disciple, is like unto a lofty tower, up which a haughty fool has climbed. Thereon he sits in prideful solitude and unperceived by any but himself.

False learning is rejected by the Wise, and scattered to the Winds by the good Law. Its wheel revolves for all, the humble and the proud. The "Doctrine of the Eye"[57] is for

---

[54] From *Shen-hsiu's* Doctrine, who teaches that the human mind is like a mirror which attracts and reflects every atom of dust, and has to be, like that mirror, watched over and dusted every day. *Shen-hsiu* was the sixth Patriarch of North China who taught the esoteric doctrine of Bodhidharma.

[55] The reincarnating Ego is called by the Northern Buddhists the "true man," who becomes in union with his Higher-Self—a Buddha.

[56] "Buddha" means "Enlightened."

[57] The *exoteric* Buddhism of the masses.

the crowd, the "Doctrine of the Heart," for the elect. The first repeat in pride: "Behold, I know," the last, they who in humbleness have garnered, low confess, "thus have I heard"[58].

"Great Sifter" is the name of the "Heart Doctrine," O disciple.

The wheel of the good Law moves swiftly on. It grinds by night and day. The worthless husks it drives from out the golden grain, the refuse from the flour. The hand of Karma guides the wheel; the revolutions mark the beatings of the Karmic heart.

True knowledge is the flour, false learning is the husk. If thou would'st eat the bread of Wisdom, thy flour thou hast to knead with Amrita's[59] clear waters. But if thou kneadest husks with Mâyâ's dew, thou canst create but food for the black doves of death, the birds of birth, decay and sorrow.

If thou art told that to become Arhan thou hast to cease to love all beings—tell them they lie.

If thou art told that to gain liberation thou hast to hate thy mother and disregard thy son; to disavow thy father

---

[58] The usual formula that precedes the Buddhist Scriptures, meaning, that that which follows is what has been recorded by direct oral tradition from Buddha and the Arhats.

[59] Immortality.

and call him "householder"[60]; for man and beast all pity to renounce—tell them their tongue is false.

Thus teach the Tîrthikas, the unbelievers.[61]

If thou art taught that sin is born of action and bliss of absolute inaction, then tell them that they err. Non-permanence of human action; deliverance of mind from thraldom by the cessation of sin and faults, are not for "Deva Egos."[62] Thus saith the "Doctrine of the Heart."

The Dharma of the "Eye" is the embodiment of the external, and the non-existing.

The Dharma of the "Heart" is the embodiment of Bodhi,[63] the Permanent and Everlasting.

The Lamp burns bright when wick and oil are clean. To make them clean a cleaner is required. The flame feels not the process of the cleaning. "The branches of a tree are shaken by the wind; the trunk remains unmoved."

Both action and inaction may find room in thee; thy body agitated, thy mind tranquil, thy Soul as limpid as a mountain lake.

---

[60] Rathapâla the great Arhat thus addresses his father in the legend called *Rathapâla Sûtrasanne.* But as all such legends are allegorical (*e.g.* Rathapâla's father has a mansion with *seven doors*) hence the reproof, to those who accept them *literally.*

[61] Brahman ascetics.

[62] The reincarnating Ego.

[63] True, divine Wisdom.

Would'st thou become a Yogi of "Time's Circle"? Then, O Lanoo:—

Believe thou not that sitting in dark forests, in proud seclusion and apart from men; believe thou not that life on roots and plants, that thirst assuaged with snow from the great Range—believe thou not, O Devotee, that this will lead thee to the goal of final liberation.

Think not that breaking bone, that rending flesh and muscle, unites thee to thy "silent Self"[64]. Think not, that when the sins of thy gross form are conquered, O Victim of thy Shadows[65], thy duty is accomplished by nature and by man.

The blessed ones have scorned to do so. The Lion of the Law, the Lord of Mercy,[66] perceiving the true cause of human woe, immediately forsook the sweet but selfish rest of quiet wilds. From Âranyaka[67] He became the Teacher of mankind. After Julai[68] had entered the Nirvâna, He preached on mount and plain, and held discourses in the cities, to Devas, men and gods[69].

---

[64] The "Higher Self" the "seventh" principle.

[65] Our physical bodies are called "Shadows" in the mystic schools.

[66] Buddha.

[67] A hermit who retires to the jungles and lives in a forest, when becoming a Yogi.

[68] *Julai* the Chinese name for Tathâgata, a title applied to every Buddha.

[69] All the Northern and Southern traditions agree in showing Buddha quitting his solitude as soon as he had resolved the problem of life—*i.e.*, received the inner enlightenment—and teaching mankind publicly.

Sow kindly acts and thou shalt reap their fruition. Inaction in a deed of mercy becomes an action in a deadly sin.

Thus saith the Sage.

Shalt thou abstain from action? Not so shall gain thy soul her freedom. To reach Nirvâna one must reach Self-Knowledge, and Self-Knowledge is of loving deeds the child.

Have patience, Candidate, as one who fears no failure, courts no success. Fix thy Soul's gaze upon the star whose ray thou art[70], the flaming star that shines within the lightless depths of ever-being, the boundless fields of the Unknown.

Have perseverance as one who doth for evermore endure. Thy shadows live and vanish[71]; that which in thee shall live for ever, that which in thee *knows*, for it is knowledge[72], is not of fleeing life: it is the man that was, that is, and will be, for whom the hour shall never strike.

If thou would'st reap sweet peace and rest, Disciple, sow with the seeds of merit the fields of future harvests. Accept the woes of birth.

---

[70] Every spiritual Ego is a ray of a "Planetary Spirit" according to esoteric teaching.

[71] "Personalities" or *physical bodies* called "shadows" are evanescent.

[72] *Mind* (*Manas*) the thinking Principle or Ego in man, is referred to "Knowledge" itself, because the human *Egos* are called *Mânasa-putras* the sons of (universal) Mind.

Step out from sunlight into shade, to make more room for others. The tears that water the parched soil of pain and sorrow, bring forth the blossoms and the fruits of Karmic retribution. Out of the furnace of man's life and its black smoke, winged flames arise, flames purified, that soaring onward, 'neath the Karmic eye, weave in the end the fabric glorified of the three vestures of the Path[73].

These vestures are: Nirmânakâya, Sambhogakâya, and Dharmakâya, robe Sublime[74].

The *Shangna* robe[75], 'tis true, can purchase light eternal. The Shangna robe alone gives the Nirvâna of destruction; it stops rebirth, but, O Lanoo, it also kills—compassion. No longer can the perfect Buddhas, who don the Dharmakâya glory, help man's salvation. Alas! shall selves be sacrificed to *Self*; mankind, unto the weal of Units?

Know, O beginner, this is the *Open* Path, the way to selfish bliss, shunned by the Bodhisattvas of the "Secret Heart," the Buddhas of Compassion.

---

73 *Vide* Part III. Glossary, paragraph 34 *et seq.*

74 *Ibid.*

75 The *Shangna* robe, from Shangnavasu of Râjagriha the third great Arhat or "Patriarch" as the Orientalists call the hierarchy of the 33 Arhats who spread Buddhism. "Shangna robe" means metaphorically, the acquirement of Wisdom with which the Nirvâna of destruction (of *personality*) is entered. Literally, the "initiation robe" of the Neophytes. Edkins states that this "grass cloth" was brought to China from Tibet in the Tong Dynasty. "When an Arhan is born this plant is found growing in a clean spot" says the Chinese as also the Tibetan legend.

To live to benefit mankind is the first step. To practise the six glorious virtues[76] is the second.

To don Nirmânakâya's humble robe is to forego eternal bliss for Self, to help on man's salvation. To reach Nirvâna's bliss, but to renounce it, is the supreme, the final step—the highest on Renunciation's Path.

Know, O Disciple, this is the *Secret* Path, selected by the Buddhas of Perfection, who sacrificed The SELF to weaker Selves.

Yet, if the "Doctrine of the Heart" is too high-winged for thee. If thou need'st help thyself and fearest to offer help to others,—then, thou of timid heart, be warned in time: remain content with the "Eye Doctrine" of the Law. Hope still. For if the "Secret Path" is unattainable this "day," it is within thy reach "to-morrow."[77]. Learn that no efforts, not the smallest—whether in right or wrong direction—can vanish from the world of causes. E'en wasted smoke remains not traceless. "A harsh word uttered in past lives, is not destroyed but ever comes again."[78] The pepper plant will not give birth to roses, nor the sweet jessamine's silver star to thorn or thistle turn.

[76] To "practise the Pâramitâ Path" means to become a Yogi with a view of becoming an ascetic.

[77] "To-morrow" means the following rebirth or reincarnation.

[78] Precepts of the Prasanga School.

Thou canst create this "day" thy chances for thy "morrow." In the "Great Journey,"[79] causes sown each hour bear each its harvest of effects, for rigid Justice rules the World. With mighty sweep of never erring action, it brings to mortals lives of weal or woe, the Karmic progeny of all our former thoughts and deeds.

Take then as much as merit hath in store for thee, O thou of patient heart. Be of good cheer and rest content with fate. Such is thy Karma, the Karma of the cycle of thy births, the destiny of those, who, in their pain and sorrow, are born along with thee, rejoice and weep from life to life, chained to thy previous actions.

* * *

Act thou for them to "day," and they will act for thee "to morrow."

'Tis from the bud of Renunciation of the Self, that springeth the sweet fruit of final Liberation.

To perish doomed is he, who out of fear of Mâra refrains from helping man, lest he should act for Self. The pilgrim who would cool his weary limbs in running waters, yet dares not plunge for terror of the stream, risks to succumb from heat. Inaction based on selfish fear can bear but evil fruit.

---

[79] "Great Journey" or the whole complete cycle of existences, in one "Round."

The Selfish devotee lives to no purpose. The man who does not go through his appointed work in life—has lived in vain.

Follow the wheel of life; follow the wheel of duty to race and kin, to friend and foe, and close thy mind to pleasures as to pain. Exhaust the law of Karmic retribution. Gain Siddhis for thy future birth.

If Sun thou can'st not be, then be the humble planet. Aye, if thou art debarred from flaming like the noon-day Sun upon the snow-capped mount of purity eternal, then choose, O Neophyte, a humbler course.

Point out the "Way"—however dimly, and lost among the host—as does the evening star to those who tread their path in darkness.

Behold Migmar,[80] as in his crimson veils his "Eye" sweeps over slumbering Earth. Behold the fiery aura of the "Hand" of Lhagpa[81] extended in protecting love over the heads of his ascetics. Both are now servants to Nyima[82] left in his absence silent watchers in the night. Yet both in Kalpas past were bright Nyimas, and may in future "Days" again become two Suns. Such are the falls and rises of the Karmic Law in nature.

---

[80] Mars.

[81] Mercury.

[82] The Sun. *Nyima*, the Sun in Tibetan Astrology. *Migmar* or Mars is symbolized by an "Eye," and *Lhagpa* or Mercury by a "Hand."

Be, O Lanoo, like them. Give light and comfort to the toiling pilgrim, and seek out him who knows still less than thou; who in his wretched desolation sits starving for the bread of Wisdom and the bread which feeds the shadow, without a Teacher, hope or consolation, and—let him hear the Law.

Tell him, O Candidate, that he who makes of pride and self-regard bond-maidens to devotion; that he, who cleaving to existence, still lays his patience and submission to the Law, as a sweet flower at the feet of Shakya-Thub-pa,[83] becomes a *Srotâpatti*[84] in this birth. The Siddhis of perfection may loom far, far away; but the first step is taken, the stream is entered, and he may gain the eye-sight of the mountain eagle, the hearing of the timid doe.

Tell him, O Aspirant, that true devotion may bring him back the knowledge, that knowledge which was his in former births. The deva-sight and deva-hearing are not obtained in one short birth.

Be humble, if thou would'st attain to Wisdom.

Be humbler still, when Wisdom thou hast mastered.

---

83 Buddha.

84 *Srotâpatti* or "he who enters in the stream" of Nirvâna, unless he reaches the goal owing to some exceptional reasons, can rarely attain Nirvâna in one birth. Usually a Chela is said to begin the ascending effort in one life and end or reach it only in his seventh succeeding birth.

Be like the Ocean which receives all streams and rivers. The Ocean's mighty calm remains unmoved; it feels them not.

Restrain by thy Divine thy lower Self.

Restrain by the Eternal the Divine.

Aye, great is he, who is the slayer of desire.

Still greater he, in whom the Self Divine has slain the very knowledge of desire.

Guard thou the Lower lest it soil the Higher.

The way to final freedom is within thy self.

That way begins and ends outside of Self[85].

Unpraised by men and humble is the mother of all Rivers, in *Tîrthika's* proud sight; empty the human form though filled with Amrita's sweet waters, in the sight of fools. Withal, the birth-place of the sacred rivers is the sacred land[86], and he who Wisdom hath, is honoured by all men.

Arhans and Sages of the boundless Vision[87] are rare as is the blossom of the Udumbara tree. Arhans are born

---

85 Meaning the personal lower "Self."

86 *Tîrthikas* are the Brahmanical Sectarians "beyond" the Himalayas called "infidels" by the Buddhists in the *sacred land*, Tibet, and *vice versa*.

87 Boundless Vision or psychic, superhuman sight. An Arhan is credited with "seeing" and knowing all at a distance as well as on the spot.

at midnight hour, together with the sacred plant of nine and seven stalks[88], the holy flower that opes and blooms in darkness, out of the pure dew and on the frozen bed of snow-capped heights, heights that are trodden by no sinful foot.

No Arhan, O Lanoo, becomes one in that birth when for the first the Soul begins to long for final liberation. Yet, O thou anxious one, no warrior volunteering fight in the fierce strife between the living and the dead[89], not one recruit can ever be refused the right to enter on the Path that leads toward the field of Battle.

For, either he shall win, or he shall fall.

Yea, if he conquers, Nirvâna shall be his. Before he casts his shadow off his mortal coil, that pregnant cause of anguish and illimitable pain—in him will men a great and holy Buddha honour.

And if he falls, e'en then he does not fall in vain; the enemies he slew in the last battle will not return to life in the next birth that will be his.

But if thou would'st Nirvâna reach, or cast the prize away[90], let not the fruit of action and inaction be thy motive, thou of dauntless heart.

---

[88] *Vide supra* 22: Shangna plant.

[89] The "living" is the immortal Higher Ego, and the "dead"—the lower *personal Ego.*

[90] *Vide infra* Part III. par. 34.

Know that the Bodhisattva who liberation changes for Renunciation to don the miseries of "Secret Life,"[91] is called, "thrice Honoured," O thou candidate for woe throughout the cycles.

The path is one, Disciple, yet in the end, twofold. Marked are its stages by four and seven Portals. At one end—bliss immediate, and at the other—bliss deferred. Both are of merit the reward: the choice is thine.

The One becomes the two, the *Open* and the *Secret*[92]. The first one leadeth to the goal, the second, to Self-Immolation.

When to the Permanent is sacrificed the Mutable, the prize is thine: the drop returneth whence it came. The *Open* path leads to the changeless change—Nirvâna, the glorious state of Absoluteness, the Bliss past human thought.

Thus, the first Path is liberation.

But Path the Second is—renunciation, and therefore called the "Path of Woe."

That *Secret* Path leads the Arhan to mental woe unspeakable; woe for the living Dead[93], and helpless pity for the men of Karmic sorrow, the fruit of Karma Sages dare not still.

---

[91] The "Secret Life" is life as a Nirmânakâya.

[92] The "Open" and the "Secret Path"—or the one taught to the layman, the exoteric and the generally accepted, and the other the Secret Path—the nature of which is explained at initiation.

[93] Men ignorant of the Esoteric truths and Wisdom are called "the living Dead."

For it is written: "teach to eschew all causes; the ripple of effect, as the great tidal wave, thou shalt let run its course."

The "Open Way," no sooner hast thou reached its goal, will lead thee to reject the Bodhisattvic body and make thee enter the thrice glorious state of Dharmakâya[94] which is oblivion of the World and men for ever.

The "Secret Way" leads also to Paranirvânic bliss—but at the close of Kalpas without number; Nirvânas gained and lost from boundless pity and compassion for the world of deluded mortals.

But it is said "The last shall be the greatest," *Samyak Sambuddha*, the Teacher of Perfection, gave up his SELF for the salvation of the World, by stopping at the threshold of Nirvâna—the pure state.

* * *

Thou hast the knowledge now concerning the two Ways. Thy time will come for choice, O thou of eager Soul, when thou hast reached the end and passed the seven Portals. Thy mind is clear. No more art thou entangled in delusive thoughts, for thou hast learnèd all. Unveiled stands truth and looks thee sternly in the face. She says:

"Sweet are the fruits of Rest and Liberation for the sake of *Self*; but sweeter still the fruits of long and bitter duty. Aye,

[94] *Vide infra* Part III. 34.

Renunciation for the sake of others, of suffering fellow men."

He, who becomes Pratyeka-Buddha[95], makes his obeisance but to his *Self.* The Bodhisattva who has won the battle, who holds the prize within his palm, yet says in his divine compassion:

"For others' sake this great reward I yield"—accomplishes the greater Renunciation.

A Saviour of the World is he.

* * *

Behold! The goal of bliss and the long Path of Woe are at the furthest end. Thou canst choose either, O aspirant to Sorrow, throughout the coming cycles!....

Om Vajrapâni hum.

---

[95] *Pratyeka Buddhas* are those Bodhisattvas who strive after and often reach the Dharmakâya robe after a series of lives. Caring nothing for the woes of mankind or to help it, but only for their own *bliss*, they enter Nirvâna and—disappear from the sight and the hearts of men. In Northern Buddhism a "Pratyeka Buddha" is a synonym of spiritual Selfishness.

FRAGMENT III

The Seven Portals

"Upâdhyâya[96], the choice is made, I thirst for Wisdom. Now hast thou rent the veil before the secret Path and taught the greater Yâna[97]. Thy servant here is ready for thy guidance."

'Tis well, Śrâvaka[98]. Prepare thyself, for thou wilt have to travel on alone. The Teacher can but point the way. The

[96] *Upâdhyâya* is a spiritual preceptor, a Guru. The Northern Buddhists choose these generally among the "*Naljor*," saintly men, learned in *gotrabhû-ñâna* and *ñâna-dassana-suddhi* teachers of the Secret Wisdom.

[97] Yâna—vehicle: thus *Mahâyâna* is the "Great Vehicle," and *Hînayâna*, the "Lesser Vehicle," the names for two schools of religious and philosophical learning in Northern Buddhism.

[98] *Śrâvaka*—a listener, or student who attends to the religious instructions. From the root "*Śru*." When from theory they go into practice or performance of asceticism, they become *Śramanas*, "exercisers," from *Śrama*, action. As Hardy shows, the two appellations answer to the words *akoustikoi* and *asketai* of the Greeks.

Path is one for all, the means to reach the goal must vary with the Pilgrims.

Which wilt thou choose, O thou of dauntless heart? The Samtan[99] of "eye Doctrine," four-fold Dhyâna, or thread thy way through Pâramitâs[100], six in number, noble gates of virtue leading to Bodhi and to Prajñâ, seventh step of Wisdom?

The rugged Path of four-fold Dhyâna winds on uphill. Thrice great is he who climbs the lofty top.

The Pâramitâ heights are crossed by a still steeper path. Thou hast to fight thy way through portals seven, seven strongholds held by cruel crafty Powers—passions incarnate.

Be of good cheer, Disciple; bear in mind the golden rule. Once thou hast passed the gate Srotâpatti[101], "he who the

---

[99] *Samtan* (Tibetan), the same as the Sanskrit *Dhyâna*, or the state of meditation, of which there are four degrees.

[100] *Pâramitâs*, the six transcendental virtues; for the priests there are *ten*.

[101] *Srotâpatti*—(lit.) "he who has entered the stream" that leads to the Nirvânic ocean. This name indicates the *first* Path. The name of the *second* is the Path of *Sakridâgâmin*, "he who will receive birth (only) once more." The *third* is called *Anâgâmin*, "he who will be reincarnated no more," unless he so desires in order to help mankind. The *fourth* Path is known as that of *Rahat* or *Arhat*. This is the highest. An Arhat sees Nirvâna during his life. For him it is no post-mortem state, but *Samâdhi*, during which he experiences all Nirvânic bliss. (How little one can rely upon the Orientalists for the exact words and meaning,

stream hath entered"; once thy foot hath pressed the bed of the Nirvânic stream in this or any future life, thou hast but seven other births before thee, O thou of adamantine Will.

Look on. What see'st thou before thine eye, O aspirant to god-like Wisdom?

"The cloak of darkness is upon the deep of matter; within its folds I struggle. Beneath my gaze it deepens, Lord; it is dispelled beneath the waving of thy hand. A shadow moveth, creeping like the stretching serpent coils.... It grows, swells out and disappears in darkness."

It is the shadow of thyself outside the Path, cast on the darkness of thy sins.

"Yea, Lord; I see the PATH; its foot in mire, its summits lost in glorious light Nirvânic. And now I see the ever narrowing Portals on the hard and thorny way to Jñâna."[102]

Thou seest well, Lanoo. These Portals lead the aspirant across the waters on "to the other shore"[103]. Each Portal

---

is instanced in the case of three "alleged" authorities. Thus the four names just explained are given by R. Spence Hardy as: 1. Sowân; 2. Sakradâgâmi; 3. Anâgâmi, and 4. Arya. By the Rev. J. Edkins they are given as: 1. Srôtâpanna; 2. Sagardagam; 3. Anagamin, and 4. Arhan. Schlagintweit again spells them differently, each, moreover, giving another and a new variation in the meaning of the terms.)

[102] Knowledge, Wisdom.

[103] "Arrival at the shore" is with the Northern Buddhists synonymous with reaching Nirvâna through the exercise of the six and the ten *Pâramitâs* (virtues).

hath a golden key that openeth its gate; and these keys are:—

1. Dâna, the key of charity and love immortal.

2. Shîla, the key of Harmony in word and act, the key that counterbalances the cause and the effect, and leaves no further room for Karmic action.

3. Kshânti, patience sweet, that nought can ruffle.

4. Virâg', indifference to pleasure and to pain, illusion conquered, truth alone perceived.

5. Vîrya, the dauntless energy that fights its way to the supernal TRUTH, out of the mire of lies terrestrial.

6. Dhyâna, whose golden gate once opened leads the Naljor[104] toward the realm of Sat eternal and its ceaseless contemplation.

7. Prajñâ, the key to which makes of a man a god, creating him a Bodhisattva, son of the Dhyânis.

Such to the Portals are the golden keys.

Before thou canst approach the last, O weaver of thy freedom, thou hast to master these Pâramitâs of perfection—the virtues transcendental six and ten in number—along the weary Path.

---

[104] A saint, an adept.

For, O Disciple! Before thou wert made fit to meet thy Teacher face to face, thy MASTER light to light, what wert thou told?

Before thou canst approach the foremost gate thou hast to learn to part thy body from thy mind, to dissipate the shadow, and to live in the eternal. For this, thou hast to live and breathe in all, as all that thou perceivest breathes in thee; to feel thyself abiding in all things, all things in SELF.

Thou shalt not let thy senses make a playground of thy mind.

Thou shalt not separate thy being from BEING, and the rest, but merge the Ocean in the drop, the drop within the Ocean.

So shalt thou be in full accord with all that lives; bear love to men as though they were thy brother-pupils, disciples of one Teacher, the sons of one sweet mother.

Of teachers there are many; the MASTER-SOUL is one[105], Alaya, the Universal Soul. Live in that MASTER as Its ray in thee. Live in thy fellows as they live in It.

Before thou standest on the threshold of the Path; before thou crossest the foremost Gate, thou hast to merge the two into the One and sacrifice the personal to SELF

---

105 The "MASTER-SOUL" is *Alaya*, the Universal Soul or Âtman, each man having a ray of it in him and being supposed to be able to identify himself with and to merge himself into it.

impersonal, and thus destroy the "path" between the two—*Antahkarana*[106].

Thou hast to be prepared to answer Dharma, the stern law, whose voice will ask thee at thy first, at thy initial step:

"Hast thou complied with all the rules, O thou of lofty hopes?"

"Hast thou attuned thy heart and mind to the great mind and heart of all mankind? For as the sacred River's roaring voice whereby all Nature-sounds are echoed back[107], so must the heart of him 'who in the stream would enter,'

---

106 *Antahkarana* is the lower *Manas*, the Path of communication or communion between the personality and the higher *Manas* or human Soul. At death it is destroyed as a Path or medium of communication, and its remains survive in a form as the *Kâmarûpa*—the "shell."

107 The Northern Buddhists, and all Chinamen, in fact, find in the deep roar of some of the great and sacred rivers the key-note of Nature. Hence the simile. It is a well-known fact in Physical Science, as well as in Occultism, that the aggregate sound of Nature—such as heard in the roar of great rivers, the noise produced by the waving tops of trees in large forests, or that of a city heard at a distance—is a definite single tone of quite an appreciable pitch. This is shown by physicists and musicians. Thus Prof. Rice (*Chinese Music*) shows that the Chinese recognized the fact thousands of years ago by saying that "the waters of the Hoang-ho rushing by, intoned the *kung*" called "the great tone" in Chinese music; and he shows this tone corresponding with the F, "considered by modern physicists to be the actual tonic of Nature." Professor B. Silliman mentions it, too, in his *Principles of Physics*, saying that "this tone is held to be the middle F of the piano; which may, therefore, be considered the key-note of Nature."

thrill in response to every sigh and thought of all that lives and breathes."

Disciples may be likened to the strings of the soul-echoing *Vînâ*; mankind, unto its sounding board; the hand that sweeps it to the tuneful breath of the great world-soul. The string that fails to answer 'neath the Master's touch in dulcet harmony with all the others, breaks—and is cast away. So the collective minds of *Lanoo-Śrâvakas*. They have to be attuned to the Upâdhyâya's mind—one with the Over-Soul—or, break away.

Thus do the "Brothers of the Shadow"—the murderers of their Souls, the dread Dad-Dugpa clan[108].

Hast thou attuned thy being to Humanity's great pain, O candidate for light?

Thou hast?... Thou mayest enter. Yet, ere thou settest foot upon the dreary Path of sorrow, 'tis well thou should'st first learn the pitfalls on thy way.

* * *

[108] The *Bons* or *Dugpas*, the sect of the "Red Caps," are regarded as the most versed in sorcery. They inhabit Western and little Tibet and Bhutan. They are all Tântrikas. It is quite ridiculous to find Orientalists who have visited the borderlands of Tibet, such as Schlagintweit and others, confusing the rites and disgusting practices of these with the religious beliefs of the Eastern Lamas, the "Yellow Caps," and their *Naljors* or holy men. The following is an instance.

Armed with the key of Charity, of love and tender mercy, thou art secure before the gate of Dâna, the gate that standeth at the entrance of the path.

Behold, O happy Pilgrim! The portal that faceth thee is high and wide, seems easy of access. The road that leads therethrough is straight and smooth and green. 'Tis like a sunny glade in the dark forest depths, a spot on earth mirrored from Amitâbha's paradise. There, nightingales of hope and birds of radiant plumage sing perched in green bowers, chanting success to fearless Pilgrims. They sing of Bodhisattvas' virtues five, the fivefold source of Bodhi power, and of the seven steps in Knowledge.

Pass on! For thou hast brought the key; thou art secure.

And to the second gate the way is verdant too. But it is steep and winds up hill; yea, to its rocky top. Grey mists will over-hang its rough and stony height, and all be dark beyond. As on he goes, the song of hope soundeth more feeble in the pilgrim's heart. The thrill of doubt is now upon him; his step less steady grows.

Beware of this, O candidate! Beware of fear that spreadeth, like the black and soundless wings of midnight bat, between the moonlight of thy Soul and thy great goal that loometh in the distance far away.

Fear, O disciple, kills the will and stays all action. If lacking in the Śîla virtue,—the pilgrim trips, and Karmic pebbles bruise his feet along the rocky path.

Be of sure foot, O candidate. In Kshânti's[109] essence bathe thy Soul; for now thou dost approach the portal of that name, the gate of fortitude and patience.

Close not thine eyes, nor lose thy sight of Dorje[110]; Mâra's arrows ever smite the man who has not reached Virâga[111].

Beware of trembling. 'Neath the breath of fear the key of Kshânti rusty grows: the rusty key refuseth to unlock.

The more thou dost advance, the more thy feet pitfalls will meet. The path that leadeth on, is lighted by one fire—the light of daring, burning in the heart. The more one dares, the more he shall obtain. The more he fears, the more that light shall pale—and that alone can guide. For as the lingering sunbeam, that on the top of some tall mountain

---

[109] Kshânti, "patience," *vide supra* the enumeration of the golden keys.

[110] *Dorje* is the Sanskrit *Vajra*, a weapon or instrument in the hands of some gods (the Tibetan *Dragshed*, the *Devas* who protect men), and is regarded as having the same occult power of repelling evil influences by purifying the air as Ozone in chemistry. It is also a *Mudrâ* a gesture and posture used in sitting for meditation. It is, in short, a symbol of power over invisible evil influences, whether as a posture or a talisman. The *Bons* or *Dugpas*, however, having appropriated the symbol, misuse it for purposes of Black Magic. With the "Yellow Caps," or *Gelugpas*, it is a symbol of power, as the Cross is with the Christians, while it is in no way more "superstitious." With the *Dugpas*, it is like the *double triangle reversed*, the sign of sorcery.

[111] *Virâga* is that feeling of absolute indifference to the objective universe, to pleasure and to pain. "Disgust" does not express its meaning, yet it is akin to it.

shines, is followed by black night when out it fades, so is heart-light. When out it goes, a dark and threatening shade will fall from thine own heart upon the path, and root thy feet in terror to the spot.

Beware, disciple, of that lethal shade. No light that shines from Spirit can dispel the darkness of the nether Soul, unless all selfish thought has fled therefrom, and that the pilgrim saith: "I have renounced this passing frame; I have destroyed the cause: the shadows cast can, as effects, no longer be."

For now the last great fight, the final war between the *Higher* and the *Lower* Self, hath taken place. Behold, the very battlefield is now engulphed in the great war, and is no more.

But once that thou hast passed the gate of Kshânti, step the third is taken. Thy body is thy slave. Now, for the fourth prepare, the Portal of temptations which do ensnare the *inner* man.

Ere thou canst near that goal, before thine hand is lifted to upraise the fourth gate's latch, thou must have mustered all the mental changes in thy Self and slain the army of the thought sensations that, subtle and insidious, creep unasked within the Soul's bright shrine.

If thou would'st not be slain by them, then must thou harmless make thy own creations, the children of thy thoughts, unseen, impalpable, that swarm round humankind, the progeny and heirs to man and his terrestrial spoils. Thou hast to study the voidness of the seeming full, the fulness of the seeming void. O fearless Aspirant, look deep within the well of thine own heart, and answer. Knowest thou of Self the powers, O thou perceiver of external shadows?

If thou dost not—then art thou lost.

For, on Path fourth, the lightest breeze of passion or desire will stir the steady light upon the pure white walls of Soul. The smallest wave of longing or regret for Mâyâ's gifts illusive, along *Antahkarana*—the path that lies between thy Spirit and thy self, the highway of sensations, the rude arousers of *Ahankâra*[112]—a thought as fleeting as the lightning flash will make thee thy three prizes forfeit—the prizes thou hast won.

For know, that the ETERNAL knows no change.

"The eight dire miseries forsake for evermore. If not, to wisdom, sure, thou can'st not come, nor yet to liberation," saith the great Lord, the Tathâgata of perfection, "he who has followed in the footsteps of his predecessors."[113].

Stern and exacting is the virtue of Virâga. If thou its path would'st master, thou must keep thy mind and thy perceptions far freer than before from killing action.

---

[112] *Ahankâra*—the "I" or feeling of one's personality, the "I-am-ness."

[113] "One who walks in the steps of his predecessors" or "those who came before him," is the true meaning of the name *Tathâgata*.

Thou hast to saturate thyself with pure Alaya, become as one with Nature's Soul-Thought. At one with it thou art invincible; in separation, thou becomest the playground of Samvriti[114], origin of all the world's delusions.

All is impermanent in man except the pure bright essence of Alaya. Man is its crystal ray; a beam of light immaculate within, a form of clay material upon the lower surface. That beam is thy life-guide and thy true Self, the Watcher and the silent Thinker, the victim of thy lower Self. Thy Soul cannot be hurt but through thy erring body; control and master both, and thou art safe when crossing to the nearing "Gate of Balance."

Be of good cheer, O daring pilgrim "to the other shore." Heed not the whisperings of Mâra's hosts; wave off the tempters, those ill-natured Sprites, the jealous Lhamayin[115] in endless space.

---

[114] *Samvriti* is that one of the two truths which demonstrates the illusive character or emptiness of all things. It is *relative* truth in this case. The *Mahâyâna* school teaches the difference between these two truths—*Paramârthasatya* and *Samvritisatya* (Satya, "truth"). This is the bone of contention between the *Mâdhyamikas* and the *Yogâchâras*, the former denying and the latter affirming that every object exists owing to a previous cause or by a concatenation. The *Mâdhyamikas* are the great Nihilists and Deniers, for whom everything is *parikalpita*, an illusion and an error in the world of thought and the subjective, as much as in the objective universe. The *Yogâchâras* are the great spiritualists. *Samvriti*, therefore, as only relative truth, is the origin of all illusion.

[115] *Lhamayin* are elementals and evil spirits adverse to men and their enemies.

Hold firm! Thou nearest now the middle portal, the gate of Woe, with its ten thousand snares.

Have mastery o'er thy thoughts, O striver for perfection, if thou would'st cross its threshold.

Have mastery o'er thy Soul, O seeker after truths undying, if thou would'st reach the goal.

Thy Soul-gaze centre on the One Pure Light, the Light that is free from affection, and use thy golden Key....

* * *

The dreary task is done, thy labour well-nigh o'er. The wide abyss that gaped to swallow thee is almost spanned....

* * *

Thou hast now crossed the moat that circles round the gate of human passions. Thou hast now conquered Mâra and his furious host.

Thou hast removed pollution from thine heart and bled it from impure desire. But, O thou glorious combatant, thy task is not yet done. Build high, Lanoo, the wall that shall hedge in the Holy Isle,[116] the dam that will protect thy mind from pride and satisfaction at thoughts of the great feat achieved.

---

[116] The Higher Ego, or Thinking Self.

A sense of pride would mar the work. Aye, build it strong, lest the fierce rush of battling waves, that mount and beat its shore from out the great World Mâyâ's Ocean, swallow up the pilgrim and the isle—yea, even when the victory's achieved.

Thine "Isle" is the deer, thy thoughts the hounds that weary and pursue his progress to the stream of Life. Woe to the deer that is o'ertaken by the barking fiends before he reach the Vale of Refuge—Jñâna Mârga, "path of pure knowledge" named.

Ere thou canst settle in Jñâna Mârga[117] and call it thine, thy Soul has to become as the ripe mango fruit: as soft and sweet as its bright golden pulp for others' woes, as hard as that fruit's stone for thine own throes and sorrows, O Conqueror of Weal and Woe.

Make hard thy Soul against the snares of *Self*; deserve for it the name of "Diamond-Soul."[118].

For, as the diamond buried deep within the throbbing heart of earth can never mirror back the earthly lights; so are thy mind and Soul; plunged in Jñâna Mârga, these must mirror nought of Mâyâ's realm illusive.

---

[117] *Jñâna-Mârga* is the "Path of *Jñâna*," literally; or the *Path of pure knowledge*, of *Paramârtha* or (Sanskrit) *Svasamvedana* "the self-evident or self-analysing reflection."

[118] *Vide* Glossary of Part II., Number 4. "Diamond-Soul" or *Vajradhara* presides over the *Dhyâni-Buddhas.*

When thou hast reached that state, the Portals that thou hast to conquer on the Path fling open wide their gates to let thee pass, and Nature's strongest mights possess no power to stay thy course. Thou wilt be master of the sevenfold Path: but not till then, O candidate for trials passing speech.

Till then, a task far harder still awaits thee: thou hast to feel thyself ALL-THOUGHT, and yet exile all thoughts from out thy Soul.

Thou hast to reach that fixity of mind in which no breeze, however strong, can waft an earthly thought within. Thus purified, the shrine must of all action, sound, or earthly light be void; e'en as the butterfly, o'ertaken by the frost, falls lifeless at the threshold—so must all earthly thoughts fall dead before the fane.

Behold it written:

"Ere the gold flame can burn with steady light, the lamp must stand well guarded in a spot free from all wind."[119] Exposed to shifting breeze, the jet will flicker and the quivering flame cast shades deceptive, dark and ever-changing, on the Soul's white shrine.

And then, O thou pursuer of the truth, thy Mind-Soul will become as a mad elephant, that rages in the jungle. Mistaking forest trees for living foes, he perishes in his

---

[119] *Bhagavadgîtâ.*

attempts to kill the ever-shifting shadows dancing on the wall of sunlit rocks.

Beware, lest in the care of Self thy Soul should lose her foothold on the soil of Deva-knowledge.

Beware, lest in forgetting SELF, thy Soul lose o'er its trembling mind control, and forfeit thus the due fruition of its conquests.

Beware of change! For change is thy great foe. This change will fight thee off, and throw thee back, out of the Path thou treadest, deep into viscous swamps of doubt.

Prepare, and be forewarned in time. If thou hast tried and failed, O dauntless fighter, yet lose not courage: fight on and to the charge return again, and yet again.

The fearless warrior, his precious life-blood oozing from his wide and gaping wounds, will still attack the foe, drive him from out his stronghold, vanquish him, ere he himself expires. Act then, all ye who fail and suffer, act like him; and from the stronghold of your Soul, chase all your foes away—ambition, anger, hatred, e'en to the shadow of desire—when even you have failed...

Remember, thou that fightest for man's liberation[120], each failure is success, and each sincere attempt wins

[120] This is an allusion to a well-known belief in the East (as in the West, too, for the matter of that) that every additional Buddha or Saint is a new soldier in the army of those who work for the liberation

its reward in time. The holy germs that sprout and grow unseen in the disciple's soul, their stalks wax strong at each new trial, they bend like reeds but never break, nor can they e'er be lost. But when the hour has struck they blossom forth[121]...

* * *

But if thou cam'st prepared, then have no fear.

* * *

Henceforth thy way is clear right through the *Vîrya* gate, the fifth one of the Seven Portals. Thou art now on the way that leadeth to the Dhyâna haven, the sixth, the Bodhi Portal.

---

or salvation of mankind. In Northern Buddhist countries, where the doctrine of *Nirmânakâyas*—those *Bodhisattvas* who renounce well-earned Nirvâna or the *Dharmakâya* vesture (both of which shut them out for ever from the world of men) in order to invisibly assist mankind and lead it finally to Paranirvâna—is taught, every new *Bodhisattva* or initiated great Adept is called the "liberator of mankind." The statement made by Schlagintweit in his "*Buddhism in Tibet*" to the effect that *Prulpai Ku* or "Nirmânakâya" is "the *body* in which the Buddhas or Bodhisattvas appear upon earth to teach men"—is absurdly inaccurate and explains nothing.

[121] A reference to human passions and sins which are slaughtered during the trials of the novitiate, and serve as well-fertilized soil in which "holy germs" or seeds of transcendental virtues may germinate. Pre-existing or *innate* virtues, talents or gifts are regarded as having been acquired in a previous birth. Genius is without exception a talent or aptitude brought from another birth.

The Dhyâna gate is like an alabaster vase, white and transparent; within there burns a steady golden fire, the flame of Prajñâ that radiates from Âtman.

Thou art that vase.

Thou hast estranged thyself from objects of the senses, travelled on the "Path of seeing," on the "Path of hearing," and standest in the light of Knowledge. Thou hast now reached Titikshâ state[122].

O Naljor thou art safe.

* * *

Know, Conqueror of Sins, once that a Sowanee[123] hath cross'd the seventh Path, all Nature thrills with joyous awe and feels subdued. The silver star now twinkles out the news to the night-blossoms, the streamlet to the pebbles ripples out the tale; dark ocean-waves will roar it to the rocks surf-bound, scent-laden breezes sing it to the vales, and stately pines mysteriously whisper: "A Master has arisen, a master of the day."[124].

---

122 *Titikshâ* is the fifth state of *Râja Yoga*—one of supreme indifference; submission, if necessary, to what is called "pleasures and pains for all," but deriving neither pleasure nor pain from such submission—in short, the becoming physically, mentally, and morally indifferent and insensible to either pleasure or pain.

123 *Sowanee* is one who practices *Sowan*, the first path in *Jñâna*, a Srotâpatti.

124 "Day" means here a whole *Manvantara*, a period of incalculable duration.

He standeth now like a white pillar to the west, upon whose face the rising Sun of thought eternal poureth forth its first most glorious waves. His mind, like a becalmed and boundless ocean, spreadeth out in shoreless space. He holdeth life and death in his strong hand.

Yea, He is mighty. The living power made free in him, that power which is himself, can raise the tabernacle of illusion high above the gods, above great Brahm and Indra. *Now* he shall surely reach his great reward!

Shall he not use the gifts which it confers for his own rest and bliss, his well-earn'd weal and glory—he, the subduer of the great Delusion?

Nay, O thou candidate for Nature's hidden lore! If one would follow in the steps of holy Tathâgata, those gifts and powers are not for Self.

Would'st thou thus dam the waters born on Sumeru?[125] Shalt thou divert the stream for thine own sake, or send it back to its prime source along the crests of cycles?

If thou would'st have that stream of hard-earn'd knowledge, of Wisdom heaven-born, remain sweet running waters, thou should'st not leave it to become a stagnant pond.

Know, if of Amitâbha, the "Boundless Age," thou would'st become co-worker, then must thou shed the light acquired,

125 Mount Meru, the sacred mountain of the Gods.

like to the Bodhisattvas twain[126], upon the span of all three worlds[127].

Know that the stream of superhuman knowledge and the Deva-Wisdom thou hast won, must, from thyself, the channel of Alaya, be poured forth into another bed.

Know, O Naljor, thou of the Secret Path, its pure fresh waters must be used to sweeter make the Ocean's bitter waves—that mighty sea of sorrow formed of the tears of men.

Alas! when once thou hast become like the fix'd star in highest heaven, that bright celestial orb must shine from out the spatial depths for all—save for itself; give light to all, but take from none.

Alas! when once thou hast become like the pure snow in mountain vales, cold and unfeeling to the touch, warm and protective to the seed that sleepeth deep beneath its bosom—'tis now that snow which must receive the biting

---

[126] In the Northern Buddhist symbology, *Amitâbha* or "Boundless Space" (*Parabrahm*) is said to have in his paradise two *Bodhisattvas*—Kwan-shi-yin and Tashishi—who ever radiate light over the three worlds where they lived, including our own (*vide* 27), in order to help with this light (of knowledge) in the instruction of Yogis, who will, in their turn, save men. Their exalted position in *Amitâbha's* realm is due to deeds of mercy performed by the two, as such Yogis, when on earth, says the allegory.

[127] These three worlds are the three planes of being, the terrestrial, astral and the spiritual.

frost, the northern blasts, thus shielding from their sharp and cruel tooth the earth that holds the promised harvest, the harvest that will feed the hungry.

Self-doomed to live through future Kalpas,[128] unthanked and unperceived by man; wedged as a stone with countless other stones which form the "Guardian Wall"[129], such is thy future if the seventh gate thou passest. Built by the hands of many Masters of Compassion, raised by their tortures, by their blood cemented, it shields mankind, since man is man, protecting it from further and far greater misery and sorrow.

Withal man sees it not, will not perceive it, nor will he heed the word of Wisdom...for he knows it not.

But thou hast heard it, thou knowest all, O thou of eager guileless Soul..... and thou must choose. Then hearken yet again.

On Sowan's Path, O Srotâpatti,[130] thou art secure. Aye, on that Mârga,[131] where nought but darkness meets the weary

---

[128] Cycles of ages.

[129] The "Guardian Wall" or the "Wall of Protection." It is taught that the accumulated efforts of long generations of Yogis, Saints and Adepts, especially of the *Nirmânakâyas*—have created, so to say, a wall of protection around mankind, which wall shields mankind invisibly from still worse evils.

[130] Sowan and Srotâpatti are synonymous terms.

[131] Mârga—"Path."

pilgrim, where torn by thorns the hands drip blood, the feet are cut by sharp unyielding flints, and Mâra wields his strongest arms—there lies a great reward *immediately* beyond.

Calm and unmoved the Pilgrim glideth up the stream that to Nirvâna leads. He knoweth that the more his feet will bleed, the whiter will himself be washed. He knoweth well that after seven short and fleeting births Nirvâna will be his....

Such is the Dhyâna Path, the haven of the Yogi, the blessed goal that Srotâpattis crave.

Not so when he hath crossed and won the Aryahata Path.[132]

There Kleśa[133] is destroyed for ever, Tanhâ's[134] roots torn out. But stay, Disciple...Yet, one word. Canst thou destroy divine compassion? Compassion is no attribute. It is the LAW of laws—eternal Harmony, Alaya's SELF; a shoreless universal essence, the light of everlasting Right, and fitness of all things, the law of love eternal.

The more thou dost become at one with it, thy being melted in its BEING, the more thy Soul unites with that which IS, the more thou wilt become Compassion Absolute[135].

---

[132] From the Sanskrit Arhat or Arhan.

[133] *Kleśa* is the love of pleasure or of worldly enjoyment, evil or good.

[134] *Tanhâ*, the will to live, that which causes rebirth.

[135] This "compassion" must not be regarded in the same light as "God, the divine love" of the Theists. Compassion stands here as an abstract,

Such is the Ârya Path, Path of the Buddhas of perfection.

Withal, what mean the sacred scrolls which make thee say?

"Om! I believe it is not all the Arhats that get of the Nirvânic Path the sweet fruition."

"Om! I believe that the Nirvâna-Dharma is entered not by all the Buddhas"[136].

"Yea; on the Ârya Path thou art no more Srotâpatti, thou art a Bodhisattva[137]. The stream is cross'd. 'Tis true thou hast a right to Dharmakâya vesture; but Sambhogakâya is greater than a Nirvânî, and greater still is a Nirmânakâya—the Buddha of Compassion[138].

---

impersonal law whose nature, being absolute Harmony, is thrown into confusion by discord, suffering and sin.

[136] In the Northern Buddhist phraseology all the great Arhats, Adepts and Saints are called Buddhas.

[137] A *Bodhisattva* is, in the hierarchy, less than a "perfect Buddha." In the exoteric parlance these two are very much confused. Yet the innate and right popular perception, owing to that self-sacrifice, has placed a *Bodhisattva* higher in its reverence than a Buddha.

[138] This same popular reverence calls "Buddhas of Compassion" those *Bodhisattvas* who, having reached the rank of an Arhat (*i.e.*, having completed the *fourth* or *seventh* Path), refuse to pass into the Nirvânic state or "don the *Dharmakâya* robe and cross to the other shore," as it would then become beyond their power to assist men even so little as Karma permits. They prefer to remain invisibly (in Spirit, so to speak) in the world, and contribute toward man's salvation by influencing them to follow the Good Law, *i.e.*, lead them on the Path of Righteousness. It is part of the exoteric

Northern Buddhism to honour all such great characters as Saints, and to offer even prayers to them, as the Greeks and Catholics do to their Saints and Patrons; on the other hand, the esoteric teachings countenance no such thing. There is a great difference between the two teachings. The exoteric layman hardly knows the real meaning of the word *Nirmânakâya*—hence the confusion and inadequate explanations of the Orientalists. For example Schlagintweit believes that *Nirmânakâya*-body, means the physical form assumed by the Buddhas when they incarnate on earth—"the least sublime of their earthly encumbrances" (*vide "Buddhism in Tibet"*)—and he proceeds to give an entirely false view on the subject. The real teaching is, however, this:—

The three Buddhic bodies or forms are styled:—

1. *Nirmânakâya.*
2. *Sambhogakâya.*
3. *Dharmakâya.*

The first is that ethereal form which one would assume when leaving his physical he would appear in his astral body—having in addition all the knowledge of an Adept. The *Bodhisattva* develops it in himself as he proceeds on the Path. Having reached the goal and refused its fruition, he remains on Earth, as an Adept; and when he dies, instead of going into Nirvâna, he remains in that glorious body he has woven for himself, *invisible* to uninitiated mankind, to watch over and protect it.

Sambhogakâya is the same, but with the additional lustre of "three perfections," one of which is entire obliteration of all earthly concerns. The *Dharmakâya* body is that of a complete Buddha, *i.e.*, no body at all, but an ideal breath: Consciousness merged in the Universal Consciousness, or Soul devoid of every attribute. Once a Dharmakâya, an Adept or Buddha leaves behind every possible relation with, or thought for this earth. Thus, to be enabled to help humanity, an Adept who has won the right to Nirvâna, "renounces the *Dharmakâya*

Now bend thy head and listen well, O Bodhisattva—Compassion speaks and saith: "Can there be bliss when all that lives must suffer? Shalt thou be saved and hear the whole world cry?"

Now thou hast heard that which was said.

Thou shalt attain the seventh step and cross the gate of final knowledge but only to wed woe—if thou would'st be Tathâgata, follow upon thy predecessor's steps, remain unselfish till the endless end.

Thou art enlightened—Choose thy way.

* * *

Behold, the mellow light that floods the Eastern sky. In signs of praise both heaven and earth unite. And from the four-fold manifested Powers a chant of love ariseth, both from the flaming Fire and flowing Water, and from sweet-smelling Earth and rushing Wind.

Hark!... from the deep unfathomable vortex of that golden light in which the Victor bathes, ALL NATURE'S wordless voice in thousand tones ariseth to proclaim:

---

body" in mystic parlance; keeps, of the Sambhogakâya, only the great and complete knowledge, and remains in his *Nirmânakâya* body. The esoteric school teaches that Gautama Buddha with several of his Arhats is such a *Nirmânakâya*, higher than whom, on account of the great renunciation and sacrifice to mankind there is none known.

Joy unto ye, O men of Myalba[139].

A Pilgram hath returned back "from the other shore."

A new Arhan[140] is born....

Peace to all beings[141].

---

[139] *Myalba* is our earth—pertinently called "Hell," and the greatest of all Hells, by the esoteric school. The esoteric doctrine knows of no hell or place of punishment other than on a man-bearing planet or earth. *Avîchi* is a state and not a locality.

[140] Meaning that a new and additional Saviour of mankind is born, who will lead men to final Nirvâna *i.e.*, after the end of the life-cycle.

[141] This is one of the variations of the formula that invariably follows every treatise, invocation or Instruction. "Peace to all beings," "Blessings on all that Lives," &c., &c.

For more books

Please visit *classypublishing.com*